modern readers — stage 2

Mystery on Elm Street

Eduardo Amos
Elisabeth Prescher
Ernesto Pasqualin

3rd edition

Richmond

© EDUARDO AMOS, ELISABETH PRESCHER, ERNESTO PASQUALIN, 2004

Diretoria: *Paul Berry*
Gerência editorial: *Sandra Possas*
Coordenação de revisão: *Estevam Vieira Lédo Jr.*
Coordenação de produção gráfica: *André Monteiro, Maria de Lourdes Rodrigues*
Coordenação de produção industrial: *Wilson Troque*

Projeto editorial: *Véra Regina A. Maselli, Kylie Mackin*

Assistência editorial: *Gabriela Peixoto Vilanova*
Revisão: *Denise Ceron*
Projeto gráfico de miolo e capa: *Ricardo Van Steen Comunicações e Propaganda Ltda./Oliver Fuchs*
Edição de arte: *Christiane Borin*
Ilustrações de miolo e capa: *Fabiana Salomão*
Diagramação: *EXATA Editoração*
Pré-impressão: *Hélio P. de Souza Filho, Marcio H. Kamoto*
Impressão e acabamento: *BMF Gráfica e Editora*
Lote 753531
Cód 12037223

Dados Internacionais de Catalogação na Publicação (CIP)
(Câmara Brasileira do Livro, SP, Brasil)

Amos, Eduardo
 Mystery on Elm Street / Eduardo Amos, Elisabeth Prescher, Ernesto Pasqualin ; (ilustrações Fabiana Salomão) . — 3. ed. — São Paulo : Moderna, 2003. — (Modern readers ; stage 2)

 1. Inglês (Ensino fundamental) I . Prescher, Elisabeth. II. Pasqualin, Ernesto. III. Salomão, Fabiana. IV. Título. V. Série.

03-3365   CDD-372.652

Índices para catálogo sistemático:
 1. Inglês : Ensino fundamental   372.652

ISBN 85-16-03722-3

Reprodução proibida. Art. 184 do Código Penal e Lei 9.610 de 19 de fevereiro de 1998.

Todos os direitos reservados.

RICHMOND
SANTILLANA EDUCAÇÃO LTDA.
Rua Padre Adelino, 758, 3º andar — Belenzinho
São Paulo — SP — Brasil — CEP 03303-904
www.richmond.com.br
2022

Impresso no Brasil

Chapter 1

It is nine o'clock on Monday morning. The day is warm and sunny. There are no clouds in the sky.

Elm Street is already busy at eight o'clock in the morning. Many people are on the street. Mike Stewart is not. He is in his bedroom.

Mrs Stewart — Mike!
Mike — Yes, Mom.
Mrs Stewart — Where are you?
Mike — Right here, Mom. By the window.
Mrs Stewart — Time for your medicine.
Mike — Oh, no! Not again.
Mrs Stewart — Come on! It's nine o'clock.

It is ten o'clock now and Mike is still at the window.

Elm Street is very, very busy at this time.

There are cars, trucks, buses, and motorcycles on the street.

There is a bus at the bus stop in front of the drugstore. Many people are at the bus stop.

Mr Harris is Bob's father and he is a mechanic. He is in his garage. There are two cars, a small truck, and an old motorcycle in the shop. Mr Harris is under the small truck.

Mrs Benson is Jack's mother. She is in her garden.

Mrs Elliott is on the sidewalk in front of her house. She is with her baby. Mrs Elliott is Sylvia's mother.

Mike's house is between Sylvia's house and Bob's house.

There is an old abandoned house between Jack's house and the garage. At ten fifteen, a big truck is in front of the old house. There are chairs, tables, beds, sofas, and an old piano on the truck.

Mr Tennison, the mail carrier, is in front of Mike's house. He is very busy this morning. There are many letters, magazines, and postcards in his bag.

Mr Tennison — Hi, Mike!
Mike — Hello, Mr Tennison!
Mr Tennison — No school today?
Mike — No. I'm sick.

Mr Tennison — I'm sorry about that.

Mike — It's okay, Mr Tennison. I'm not too bad.

Mr Tennison — Well, here are two letters for your father and a postcard for you.

Mike — Thanks.

Mr Tennison — Are there new people in the old house? A new family?

Mike — No, just an old man.

Mr Tennison — Just one old man in that big house? Strange, very strange.

Mike — Yes, and there are many old things on that truck. Old chairs, an old table, and an old piano. Look! The old man is walking out of the house now.

Mr Tennison — Yes, he is really very strange.

monday 11.00

That old man is really weird. His clothes are dark. His eyes are strange. He is so pale.

His clothes are old. The furniture is old too.

Well, there is finally somebody in the old abandoned house.

But, who is he? Where is his family? Is he an old musician or maybe an actor? Is he a good man, or is he a crook? A crook? No, perhaps just an old man.

I have a lot of news for the kids this afternoon.

Chapter 2

At three o'clock in the afternoon, Bob, Jack, and Sylvia are in Mike's bedroom. Mike is much better and very happy because he is not alone now. His friends are happy too.

Bob — Hi, Mike!
Mike — Hi guys!
Sylvia — Are you feeling better?
Mike — Yeah, thanks.

Jack — That's good.
Mike — And school?
Bob — It's okay.
Mike — Any news?
Sylvia — There is good news and bad news.
Mike — Give me the bad news first.
Sylvia — There is a Geography test the day after tomorrow.
Mike — Oh, no! .... Well, what about the good news?
Bob — There is no homework for tomorrow.
Mike — That's great! Well guys, I have news for you too. Good news.
Sylvia — What is it? I'm curious.
Mike — Remember that old house? There is an old man there now.
Bob — Just an old man? What about his family?
Mike — There's no family. Just an old man. Isn't it strange?
Jack — Yes, very strange.
Mike — And his dark clothes are really weird.
Jack — Wow! Maybe he's crazy?
Mike — Or perhaps he's a crook.
Bob — So, what are we going to do Mike?
Mike — An investigation.
Sylvia — Cool!
Mike — Let's make a plan.
Bob — Great idea!

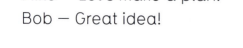

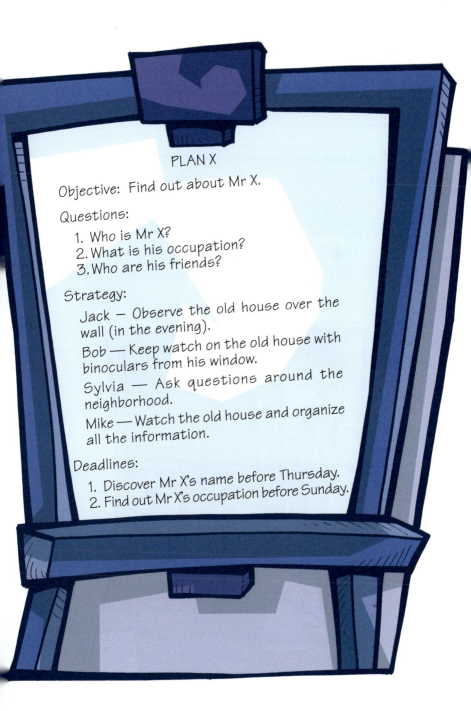

Chapter 3

It is eight-thirty in the evening. Elm Street is very quiet at this time. It is a warm night, but there are no stars in the sky, and no moon. It is very dark.

Mike and Bob are at their bedroom windows. They are talking on the telephone.

Mr X is at home. He is playing soft music on the piano.

Suddenly, a black van stops in front of the old house. A man, a woman, and a boy are in the van.

Mike — Look Bob! The old man is at the front door now.
Bob — Yeah, he is walking to the van! …. He is carrying the boy into his house!
Mike — Oh, no! The man is a kidnapper!

A minute later, Elm Street is quiet and empty.
The two boys are frightened.

It is nine-thirty and Jack is on the wall between his house and the old house.

"Hmm... There is a light in the living room now. Mr X is in the living room!

But ... another person is there too. Who is it? Is it another man? ... No, it's not a man. Maybe it's an old woman. I can't see very well from here... I know. I'll go over to that window!"

Two minutes later, Jack is in Mr X's yard. It is very dark.

Now he is near the window. What a surprise! There is a boy on a sofa in the living-room and medicine on a small table. Mr X is on a chair near the sofa.

Suddenly, there is a noise in the yard.

"Oh, no! It is a dog! It's a big black dog!"

The dog is very close to Jack.

The boy runs over to the wall and jumps. It is too late. The dog bites a hole in his pants.

It is Tuesday afternoon.

Sylvia is always very busy in the afternoon. She has Spanish classes on Mondays and Wednesdays and volleyball training on Tuesdays and Thursdays. Sylvia is not at volleyball training today. She is very busy with her investigation. She is in front of the drugstore.

"Well, no news at the grocery. No news at the garage. Let's go to the drugstore!"

Sylvia — Hello, Mr Wilson!
Mr Wilson — Oh, hello Sylvia. How are you this afternoon?
Sylvia — Fine, thanks.
Mr Wilson — Can I help you, Sylvia?
Sylvia — Hmm, well, Mr Wilson...
Mr Wilson — What's the problem, Sylvia?
Sylvia — Mr X!
Mr Wilson — Mr X? Who is Mr X?

Sylvia — The old man in the old house.
Mr Wilson — Oh, Mr MacDonald?
Sylvia — Mr MacDonald? Is that his name? Are you sure?
Mr Wilson — Yes, I'm sure.
Sylvia — Great! Thanks a lot, Mr Wilson! Bye!
Mr Wilson — Hey, wait a minute Sylvia! Kids! They are always in a hurry.

Chapter 4

The kids are in Mike's room again. It is eight o'clock in the evening and they are talking about their investigation. Jack is by the window.

Sylvia — Well guys, the name of Mr X is Mr Mac Donald.

Mike — And, here is my report and a picture.

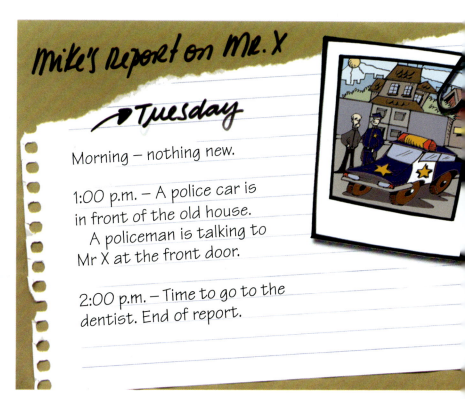

Mike's Report on Mr. X

Tuesday

Morning — nothing new.

1:00 p.m. — A police car is in front of the old house.
A policeman is talking to Mr X at the front door.

2:00 p.m. — Time to go to the dentist. End of report.

Sylvia — Hmm... Mr X and a policeman... very suspicious.

Jack — I'm sure Mr X is a kidnapper.

Bob — Here is my report. Everything is very suspicious too.

BOB'S REPORT ON MR.X

TUESDAY AFTERNOON

2:00 p.m. — The old abandoned house is quiet.

2:15 p.m. — There is someone behind the curtain in the living-room. Maybe it is Mr X.

2:30 p.m. — There is no movement in the house. I am tired. My binoculars are very heavy.

3:30 p.m. — A van is in front of the house. There are boxes on the sidewalk. A man and a woman are carrying the boxes into the house. What is in the boxes?

4:00 p.m. — The street is empty and quiet again. No van. No people. Nobody behind the curtains.

6:00 p.m. — Nothing new. End of report.

Suddenly...

Jack - Hey, look! Look at the window of the old house!

Chapter 5

It is Wednesday morning. The day is cloudy and windy.

Mike is not sick today. At twelve-thirty, he and his friends are on Elm Street. They are walking back from school.

Suddenly...

Jack — Hey, look!

Bob — What?

Jack — Over there! In front of Sylvia's house.

Sylvia — It's my mother. What's the problem?

Mike — Who's that man talking to your mother?

Sylvia — Is it Mr MacDonald?

Jack — Yes! Mr X is talking to your mother, Sylvia.

Sylvia — Maybe she is in danger.

Bob — Quick! Let's go, guys!

The kids run to Sylvia's house. They are very frightened.

Only Mrs Elliot is in the garden now. The man is not there.

Sylvia — Where is that man? Are you all right, Mom?
Mrs Elliott — Of course I am. What's the problem?
Mike — That man is dangerous, Mrs Elliott!
Jack — Maybe he is a crook!
Sylvia — Maybe he is a kidnapper!
Bob — I'm sure he is.
Mrs Elliott — Wait! Wait a minute! Look, here is an invitation for you kids.

An invitation from Mr X? Isn't he a crook? Isn't he a kidnapper? The kids are very confused. Who is the old man, then?

Sylvia — The old man is very dangerous, Mom.

Mrs Elliott — Hold on a minute! Listen to me! Mr MacDonald is a policeman. He is a sheriff.

Mike — Of course! Remember the police car in front of his house the other day.

Jack — Sure! He is a policeman.

Bob — But what about the boy?

Mrs Elliott — That's Alex, his grandson. He is sick.

Sylvia — Is he very sick?

Mrs Elliott — Well, not now. It is his birthday tomorrow. This is an invitation to his birthday party!

It is Thursday, 8:00 p.m. Mike, Sylvia, Bob, and Jack are at the party at Mr MacDonald's house. They are talking to Alex and his grandfather.

The boy is happy with his new friends. Four new friends!

The kids are happy too. But there are still some things they want to know.

Mike — Whose black van is that, Alex?

Alex — That's my father's van.

Sylvia — And the two people in the van?

Alex — Oh, they are my Mom and Dad. They are over there, near the door.

Mr MacDonald - Are you happy now, kids?

Mike — Yes, Mr MacDonald. We are very sorry.

Bob — What is the matter now, Sylvia?

Sylvia — I remember the scenes behind the curtain.

KEY WORDS

The meaning of each word corresponds to its use in the context of the story (see page number, 00)

actor (8) ator
again (4) novamente
alone (9) sozinho
a lot of (8) muito/a
already (3) já
always (16) sempre
another (3) outro
any (10) algum
back (20) de volta
before (11) antes de
behind (18) atrás
better (9) melhor
between (5) entre
birthday (22) aniversário
bite, bites (15) morder
box, boxes (18) caixa/s
bus stop (5) ponto de ônibus
busy (3) agitado; **(6)** ocupado
carry, carrying (13) carregar
clothes (8) roupas
cloud (3) nuvem
cloudy (20) nublado
crook (8) criminoso
curtain (18) cortina
danger (20) perigo
dangerous (21) perigoso
dark (8) escuro
deadline (11) prazo
empty (13) vazio
evening (11) noite

everything (18) tudo
eye (8) olho
find out (11) descobrir
frightened (13) assustado
furniture (8) mobília
go over to (14) ir até
grandfather (24) avô
grandson (23) neto
grocery (16) mercearia
guys (9) pessoal
happy (9) feliz
have, has (8) ter
heavy (18) pesado
hole (15) buraco
in front of (5) em frente
invitation (21) convite
jump, jumps (15) pular
just (7) apenas
kid (8) criança
kidnapper (13) seqüestrador
later (13) mais tarde
light (14) luz
magazine (6) revista
mail carrier (6) carteiro
make (10) fazer
many (3) muitos
maybe (8) talvez
medicine (4) remédio
moon (12) lua
much (9) muito

near (15) perto de
neighborhood (11) vizinhança
news (8) novidades
nobody (18) ninguém
noise (15) barulho
nothing (17) nada
over there (20) lá
pale (8) pálido
pants (15) calça
party (22) festa
people (3) pessoas
perhaps (8) talvez
postcard (6) cartão-postal
remember (10) lembrar-se
report (17) relatório
right here (4) bem aqui
run over to (15) correr até
scene (24) cena
see (14) ver
sick (3) doente
sidewalk (5) calçada
sky (3) céu
so (8) tão
soft (12) suave
somebody (8) alguém
someone (18) alguém
star (12) estrela
still (4) ainda
strange (7) estranho
suddenly (13) de repente
sunny (3) ensolarado
talk, talking (17) conversar
tired (18) cansado
tomorrow (10) amanhã
too (8) também
too late (15) tarde demais
truck (5) caminhão
under (5) embaixo de

walk, walking (7) andar
wall (11) muro
warm (3) quente
weird (8) estranho
who (8) quem
whose (24) de quem
windy (20) com vento
with (5) com
yard (15) quintal

Expressions

Are you all right.....? (21)
Você está bem?
Are you feeling better? (9)
Está se sentindo melhor?
Are you sure? (16)
Tem certeza?
Come on! (4) Vamos!
Cool! (10) Legal!
Hold on a minute! (23)
Espere um pouquinho
I'm not too bad! (7)
Eu não estou tão mal
I'm sorry (7) Sinto muito
in a hurry (16) com pressa
Let's go! (20) Vamos!
Listen to me! (23) Me escute!
Of course! (21) É lógico!
Quick! (20) Rápido!
Sure! (23) Claro!
Time for...! (4)
Está na hora de...
too late (15) tarde demais
Wait a minute! (21)
Espere um pouco!
What a drag! (3) Que saco!
What's the matter? (24)
Qual é o problema?

ACTIVITIES

Before Reading

1. Look at the title and picture on the front cover. Read about the story on the back cover. Now look at the words below and imagine what happens in the story.

an old abandoned house	a mysterious old man
a sick boy	a police car

2. Look at the picture of the boy on page 3. Imagine that the boy is writing a note in his diary. What is he writing?

While Reading

Chapter 1

3. Read page 3 and check your answers to 2.

4. Read pages 4 and 5. Complete the sentences with the prepositions below:

between	on	in front of
at	under	in

a. The bus stop is _____ the drugstore.
b. Mr Harris is _____ his garage.
c. Mike's house is _____ Sylvia's house and Bob's house.
d. Sylvia's mother is _____ the sidewalk.
e. There are many people _____ the bus stop.
f. Mr Harris is _____ the small truck.

5. Read pages 6 and 7. Who says these things? Write T (Mr Tennison) or M (Mike).

a. (   ) "No school today?"

b. (   ) "No, I'm sick."

c. (   ) "I'm sorry about that"

d. (   ) "Are there new people in the old house? A new family?"

e. (   ) "No, just an old man."

6. Read page 8. Complete the chart below with the information about Mr X.

APPEARANCE	Pale, strange eyes
CLOTHES	
POSSIBLE OCCUPATIONS	

Chapter 2

7. Read pages 9 and 10. What are the children planning?

8. Read page 11 and complete the chart with the responsibilities of each teenager in the plan.

Name	Responsibilities
1. Sylvia	
2. Bob	
3. Jack	
4. Mike	

Chapter 3

9. Read page 12 and describe what each of these people are doing.

a. Mike and Bob are _____

b. Mr X's _____

29

10. Go to page 13 and look at the picture. Discuss the following questions with a partner:
    a. Who are the man and the woman?
    b. Who is the boy?
    c. What is the old man doing?

11. Now read page 13 and tick the correct alternative.
    a. Mike thinks the old man is:
       (   ) a crook   (   ) a police officer
    b. The two boys are:
       (   ) curious   (   ) frightened

12. Read pages 14 and 15 and describe what Jack can see in the living room. Use the words below:

on (2)	near	in

    There is a boy _____ the sofa _____ the living room. There is medicine _____ a small table. Mr X is on a chair _____ the sofa.

13. Read page 16 and then fill in Sylvia's typical schedule during the week.

    Sylvia's typical week

	Mon	Tues	Weds	Thurs	Fri
Morning	school	school	school	school	school

    Lunch Time

	Mon	Tues	Weds	Thurs	Fri
Afternoon	Spanish	_____	Spanish	_____	Homework
	class	_____	class	_____	

14. Today isn't a typical day for Sylvia. Why not?

30

Chapter 4

15. Read pages 17 and 18 and complete the table with information about the kids' investigation.

THE INVESTIGATION

Who?	Mike	Sylvia	Jack	Bob
sees a police officer talking to Mr X.	X			
takes a photo				
sees someone behind the curtains in the old house				
sees a man and a woman carrying boxes into the old house				
finds out Mr X's name				

16. Look at the picture on page 19 and give your opinion. What is happening in the picture? Discuss with a friend.

Chapter 5

17. Look at the picture on page 20. Mr X is giving a card to Sylvia's mother. In your opinion, what is it about? Discuss your ideas with a partner.

18. Now read page 21 to 23. What is the card really about?

19. Read page 23 and answer T (True) or F (False).
   a. (   ) Sylvia thinks that Mr MacDonald is very dangerous.
   b. (   ) Mr MacDonald is a policeman.
   c. (   ) The boy is Mr MacDonald´s son.
   d. (   ) It´s the boy´s birthday today.
   e. (   ) Mr MacDonald invites the boys to the party.

31

20. Read page 24 and answer the questions.
a. Whose is the black van?
b. Who are the two people in the van?

21. Look at the picture on page 25. Compare it with the picture on page 19. Are you surprised?

After Reading (Optional Activities)

22. Imagine you receive an invitation to the boy's birthday party but you can't go. Tomorrow you already have plans. Write an e-mail. Thank him for the invitation. Explain why you can't go.

> Alex
>
> Thanks for you invitation. Sorry, I can't go.
> Tomorrow _____
> _____
> _____
> _____
> Bye

23. Do you think the boys are right to investigate Mr X?
They use binoculars and take photos. What do you think about this?